enjoying
Blueb

MW00987301

by Julie Zickefoose

Contents

Bluebirds Outside the Window   2

Species Profiles: Eastern, Western,
  and Mountain Bluebirds   5

Nest Box Design   9

Mounting and Siting the Box   10

Nest Box Monitoring   12

Nesting Schedules   13

Competitors   14

Troubleshooting Chart   16

Baffling Predators   19

Parasites and Pests   22

Bluebird Rescues   25

Enhancing Your Property   26

Native Plants for Bluebirds   31

COVER: *Male eastern bluebird photograph by Bill Thompson, III. Above: A male eastern bluebird. Photograph by Bill Thompson, III.*

ENJOYING BLUEBIRDS MORE was produced by the staff of *Bird Watcher's Digest*: Bill Thompson, III, *Editor-in-Chief, Co-Publisher, and Booklet Concept*; Andy Thompson, *Co-Publisher, BWD Press*; Jim Cirigliano, *Managing Editor*; Kyle Carlsen, *Editorial Assistant*; Claire Mullen, *Production Director*.

Bird Watcher's Digest is published by Pardson Corporation, P.O. Box 110, Marietta, OH 45750. To order additional copies of *ENJOYING BLUEBIRDS MORE*, any of our other booklets (see back cover), or for *BWD* subscription information, call us toll-free at 1-800-879-2473 or visit **birdwatchersdigest.com**. **ISBN # 1-880241-08-0.**

Bluebirds

Bluebirds not only delight us, they seem by their very presence to appeal for our help.

If there is a magic bird, it is the bluebird: breathtakingly beautiful and eager to live near us, appearing as if conjured up by a sorcerer when we offer it a simple box where it may nest. Every time I think I've decided which one I think is most beautiful, I change my mind. It's like choosing between the three shades of breathtaking blue; whichever one I'm looking at—the cobalt eastern, the ultramarine western, or the cerulean mountain—is the one I love most. How blessed we are to have these brilliant thrushes to care for all across the country!

I've been taking my children out on the bluebird nestbox trail ever since they fit into a backpack. And now both of them are taller than I. I'll never forget the morning Phoebe, then 5, and I opened a nestbox and found the bluebird eggs hatching, the squirming pink nestlings wearing eggshell hats. I held the nest for Phoebe to look into for a moment, and she watched them silently, then looked up and said, "I feel like I've been blessed."

There is no better way to witness a miracle than to peek into a bluebird nest box, no better way to achieve empathy for another species than to watch it grow up. This booklet can be a key to something miraculous, magical, and practically free.

I started monitoring and studying bluebirds in 1982, when I was living in a converted chicken house on a Connecticut estate. Wherever I've lived since, I've successfully invited bluebirds to live, too. It's no coincidence, really. Bluebirds and I like the same kind of habitat: open fields, brushy borders, meadows abounding in crickets, katydids, spiders, and caterpillars.

There were no nesting bluebirds when we arrived at Indigo Hill, our home in southeast Ohio, in 1992. In a good year, we now host six pairs, cranking out two and sometimes three broods each season. They are a gift we've given ourselves.

A pair of eastern bluebirds perches in a pasture tree. The female is a slightly paler version of the male's attractive blue and rust coloration.

SANDYSPHOTOS/WIKI

We've done what we can to welcome these birds into our habitat. I remember something Bill said when we first considered a move to Ohio. "Don't worry. Wherever we end up, we'll make our own weather." And so, it seems, we have. And sometimes we have to work around the weather that we've got.

Each spring, after freak spring snowstorms and cold snaps, when their parents can't find enough insects to feed them, I go from box to box, snatching bluebird and chickadee nestlings back from death's door. I gather them from the nest and warm them in a small cooler with a hot water bottle until they're able to come out of torpor and swallow the special bug omelet I've brought, made from scrambled egg and dried flies. It smells as nauseating as it sounds, but it's manna to a starving bird. I feed them and replace the warm, well-fed babies in the nest. I leave food for the adults to give them, and come back three more times each day to warm and feed them until the cold snap passes.

Letting nature take its course is not my style, at least where bluebird management is concerned. What I do is more fairly described as intensive bird ranching. Each life is precious to me, worth working to save. I brave swarms of mites and roiling masses of blowfly larvae to rid my tenants' nests of parasites. The reward is that bluebirds in the vicinity of my 26-box trail are now a common sight. Fall finds flocks of up to 14 adorning the power lines over rolling hay meadows. In a good year, my boxes will fledge close to 100 young bluebirds and a dozen or more Carolina chickadees and tree swallows— one potent way to make the world a more beautiful place.

I wrote this booklet with the sole intent of spreading a kind of gospel, one of taking responsibility for the birds we invite with our nest boxes. If we are to coax bluebirds to live in the artificial structures we provide, we owe it to them to make sure that the boxes are mounted not on trees or fence posts but on metal poles. And to these metal poles we must affix effective predator baffles. You'll find plans for making them here. A prospective bluebird landlord makes a commitment to monitor the nests weekly, and to intervene when (s)he's needed. Our Troubleshooting Chart will guide you through. The payoff for this landlord's commitment is an intimate look into the natural history of some of North America's most endearing and beautiful birds, a chance to come to truly know bluebirds through helping them. 🐦

ILLUSTRATION BY JULIE ZICKEFOOSE

Species Profiles

Eastern, western, and mountain bluebirds— how are they similar and how do they differ?

Thrush. A simple word, earthy, clad in muted browns. Thrushes wear earth tones, spin arias in the forest gloom. But bluebirds! Can they be thrushes? Their beauty seems an extravagance. Each of the three species flashes a different shade. At one end of the spectrum is the mountain bluebird, with its light, heavenly cerulean-turquoise. The eastern adds a touch of rose, its blue cooler, leaning toward cobalt. And richest of all is the western's blue, deep ultramarine, a neon flash in the sere grass beneath the ponderosas.

They are variations on a theme. Eastern and western might at a casual glance be mistaken for each other, but the western male's throat shines blue, where the eastern's is rusty, and the rufous breast band runs over the western's back. Female westerns have a blue-gray, rather than whitish, throat and are overall grayer and duller than eastern females.

Mountain bluebirds are longer of wing, leg, and bill than easterns or westerns, and males are unmistakable, pure pale cerulean overall. And they are broader, finding the 1½-inch entry hole that is suitable for their smaller relatives a bit

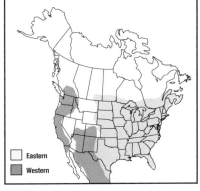

Eastern
Western

Mountain

The ranges of our three bluebird species overlap in only a few areas. Mountain bluebirds are the most strongly migratory— easterns and westerns are primarily year-round residents wherever sufficient winter food is available.

confining. A hole 1⁹/₁₆-inches suits them better and still refuses entry to starlings.

All bluebirds are birds of the open field, of grasslands with scattered patches of trees where they might find old woodpecker holes in which to nest. They take insects wherever they can find them, relying heavily on grasshoppers, crickets, and beetles, saving the softer spiders and lepidopteran larvae for younger nestlings. Of the three species, the eastern takes the most fruit, with only 68 percent of its diet made up of insects. Next is the western, with 82 percent insects and 18 percent fruit.

Most insectivorous of all is the mountain bluebird, with 92 percent of its diet made up of insects. It is the most insect-reliant of any thrush, and it is not surprising that of the three bluebird species, the mountain is the most strongly migratory. It follows its prey up the slopes of mountains in spring and back down in fall, migrating to Texas in breathtakingly large flocks. Though it employs the classic bluebird still-hunting technique of perching, then dropping to the ground for insects, the mountain bluebird hovers more while hunting. Its longer wings may make hovering easier and enable it to exploit vast treeless expanses that western bluebirds cannot.

Social creatures, bluebirds are found in family groups or flocks for most of the year, breaking up only as nesting season arrives. On the wintering grounds, flocks lead a nomadic life, seeking stands of fruiting shrubs, trees, and tangles, moving to sun-warmed fields in hope of surprising sluggish insects. Eastern bluebirds migrate only as far south as they must to find food, straggling to the southeast United States as they are pushed. They often roost together in cavities in severe weather, and nest boxes left up over the winter are sometimes filled to capacity.

Probably the single largest influence on bluebird numbers is

6

WALTER SIEGMUND/WIKI

Males at a glance. Far left: The all-blue mountain bluebird. Middle: The orange-throated eastern bluebird. This page: The blue-throated western bluebird which also has some rust on its back, unlike its eastern cousin.

weather, and severe spring weather, with freak snow or ice storms, can be disastrous. These storms strike when fruit reserves are exhausted and insects are not yet active. Like Carolina wren numbers, bluebird populations may peak, only to crash with severe late-winter weather.

Yet bluebirds seem to turn their thoughts toward nesting earlier than most birds, and the lengthening days and warming sun of February and March find them fluttering before nest holes and warbling softly. In their nesting biology, the three species are more similar than not. All three are secondary cavity users; they must rely on other species' used nesting cavities, lacking strong bills with which to excavate.

Having such exquisite plumage, bluebirds may be forgiven for expending less brilliance on song than do other thrushes. Their songs are largely composed of simple call notes strung together in short phrases that sound slightly nasal. Males, especially mountain blue-

birds, may arrive on breeding grounds before females and advertise their territories by singing from exposed perches.

Visual displays center largely around wing-waving and slow, butterfly-like flights around the nest site, accented with vigorous singing. A male may launch into the air with tail spread and legs drooping, fluttering from the cavity back to the female, then cling at the hole, poking his head in repeatedly. He may enter and call to the female from inside. Soon she follows him and inspects the cavity, while he perches nearby, waving his wings and singing.

Bluebirds fight, sometimes viciously, over nest cavities. While males attack strange males entering their territory, females attack only other females. It seems that both sexes leave their options open for mating with birds other than their partners. Conflicts can be violent. Though wing-waving

Studies have shown that adult male
bluebirds sometimes feed female offspring twice as
often as they feed males!

and chasing usually serve to rout an intruder, bluebirds occasionally roll and tumble on the ground, hammering with bills and tearing with claws. I've seen one female killed, and I nursed a male for two weeks before he was able to fly, following such battles.

When a pair at last settles down, it is the female who appears to make the final decision about where to nest. A male may show her a variety of homes before she is satisfied. Then she takes over and spends the next week or less commuting with beakfuls of soft dry grass. She packs and shapes them into a deep cup, lined with finer grasses and sometimes hair. While western and mountain bluebirds often lay six eggs, most easterns lay five pale blue eggs in the first clutch. The female alone incubates for the next 14 days, and both care for the young.

Although the popular image of bluebirds is that of steadfast monogamy, studies of eastern bluebirds have shown that the young inside a box might not all be the offspring of the pair caring for them! Extra-pair copulations are fairly frequent for both sexes, as is egg-dumping by wandering females.

Close observation of a nest box can yield surprising results. A box I watched for several hours each day had three adult males and one female tending the nestlings. No aggression was evident between the males. One would sit atop the box as another fed the young, while a third waited its turn to visit from a nearby cedar. One of the males regularly left its duties to sing at a box several hundred yards away, as if in hopes of attracting its own mate. Were they siblings? Did a shortage of females prompt the helping behavior? I'll always wonder. Helping is better documented in juvenile bluebirds, who frequently return to assist their parents in raising a second or third brood.

A strange phenomenon revealed in one recent study showed that while females showed no preference, male bluebirds feed female offspring up to twice as often as they fed males! One explanation might be that males might someday compete with their fathers for mates, while females pose no such threat. It is tempting to wonder how the males tell the sex of their young in the dark nest cavities. Are their voices different?

We are just beginning to unravel the mysteries of bluebird mating systems. Clearly, they are complex. Much of what we know from recent work has been revealed only by DNA analysis ("paternity tests"), a bit beyond the reach of most bluebird enthusiasts. But putting up even one nest box can open the door to another world of involvement and fascination in the lives of these birds. ➥

Box Design

Whether you buy or build your own bluebird box, there are several points to consider. If you'd like to build one, you can get plans from the North American Bluebird Society, P.O. Box 7844, Bloomington, IN 47407. (You can also visit **nabluebirdsociety.org** or call (812) 988-1876.) A donation to cover costs is appreciated.

If you decide to buy a box, keep the following characteristics in mind:

1. **Material:** Wood, ¾-inch or more thick, provides the best insulation from heat and cold. Cedar is naturally weather resistant. Other wood should be protected from the weather.

2. **Preparation:** Light, neutral colors of paint, stain, or clear sealer may be applied on outside of box only, and allowed to dry and air thoroughly. Pressure-treated wood contains copper arsenate and should not be used. Metal flashing tacked over cut ends of back and roof seam prevents water entry. Nails or screws, not staples, should be used to hold the box together.

3. **Access:** Side or front should swing open for monitoring and cleaning, and should be secured at bottom with a screw to prevent tampering. Top-opening boxes are hard to clean and must be mounted too low to be safe from predators if one is to look inside them.

4. **Dimensions:** Entry hole should be 1½ inches for eastern and western bluebirds; 1⁹⁄₁₆ inches wherever mountain bluebirds occur. Floor: 4 to 5½ inches square. The floor should be 8 inches below the entry hole, although slot boxes may be considerably shallower to repel house sparrows. Perches, favored by house sparrows, should be avoided.

5. **Roof:** Should be slanted, with back higher than front, and over-hanging one inch or more to keep rain

and sun out of the entry hole.

6. **Interior:** Should be free from sharp projectiles. Inside of front should be deeply scored below hole to give toehold to emerging birds.

7. **Ventilation/Drainage:** Drill holes or gaps on top of two sides for cross-ventilation. You should seal the holes with flexible weather-stripping (Mortite is one brand) in cold weather; this should be removed once the weather warms.

8. **Floor:** Should be recessed and completely covered by the sides and front of the box. Rain will seep into the seams of a floor nailed flush to the box sides.

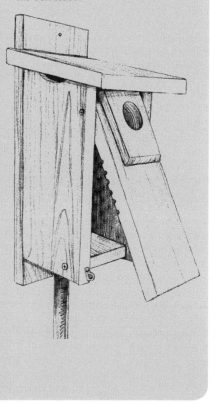

Siting the Box

I t's spring, and a pair of bluebirds is prospecting around your yard. You have a box, and you want to put it up in a hurry. Why not just nail it to a tree? At all costs, resist the temptation to bang a box onto the nearest tree or fence post. Mounting your bluebird box properly will save you future expense and heartache and possibly save the lives of the bluebirds.

It's hard to beat a 5-foot length of 1/2-inch electrical conduit (available at plumbing supply, hardware, or lumberyards) for mounting bluebird boxes. When you mount a box on free-standing pipe, you free yourself to put it wherever you like, in the best place for bluebirds. It won't rot

like wood, and its small diameter makes it easy to mount predator baffles. If you need to grease the pole to stop climbing ants, you can wipe off old and apply new grease on the non-absorbent metal. The 5-foot length lets you mount the box at eye level, which makes it easy to check. Even pipe, however, affords no protection from climbing raccoons or snakes, so you'll need to fit it with a baffle (see page 20 for plans).

There are a few ground rules for siting a bluebird box. Most important is to keep the box as far away from shrubbery and treelines as possible. House wrens, which are highly destructive competitors for boxes, are reluctant to cross open spaces. If possible, site the box 25 feet or

JULIE ZICKEFOOSE (2)

more away from cover. Bluebirds greatly appreciate additional perches in vast expanses; these perches can simply be stakes or tree limbs stuck in the ground. Adding a few places to perch can enhance a box's attractiveness at no expense.

Mount the box about five feet off the ground, or so that the bottom of the box is at your eye level. This is high enough to foil most leaping cats, and low enough to make it easy for you to monitor nests. The baffle should go as high up under the box as possible. Face the box away from prevailing winds, which generally means facing it south. If you need to fudge a little to make it easy to see the hole, the birds won't mind.

Although bluebirds appreciate boxes year-round, you'll want to have them up by February in the South and March in the North, to catch the eye of returning migrants. Keep in mind that in the winter, bluebirds often roost in boxes. I use flexible putty weatherstripping (Mortite) to caulk all ventilation holes, and I don't remove it until the weather is reliably warm. It's vital that the box stay dry inside at all times, for even an attentive bluebird mother can't save eggs or young in a soaked, cold nest.

It's a great idea to have a spare box or two on hand. If house wrens or swallows oust your bluebirds, if an old box becomes soaked, or if another bluebird pair shows up where you have but one house, you can quickly erect a spare. Where tree swallows are abundant, you may wish to pair your boxes, 15 to 25 feet apart (see "Competitors"). ✒

Open meadows are ideal sites for bluebird boxes (left). But all boxes should have pole-mounted predator baffles to maximize the safety of the nest. Below: A female eastern bluebird peeks out from the nest cavity.

Nest Box Monitoring

By keeping tabs on your bluebirds you will learn how to be a better landlord.

From the time we are very young, we're taught never to touch a young bird, or to go near a nest, for fear the parents will abandon it. On the whole, this dictum has done birds a lot of good. In truth, a parent bird's instinct to protect its young far outweighs its fear of people. Opening a nest box to check its contents can be of great benefit to bluebirds and is a matchless opportunity to learn about their nesting biology.

A bluebird box put up and never monitored is like a letter never sent. At best, bluebirds may get a brood out of it before a house wren or house sparrow takes over and fills it with nesting material, barring any other species. At worst, it may fledge broods of house sparrows, which oust and kill bluebirds wherever they find them.

Proper mounting is vital to safe box monitoring. Repeated visits to a box lay a scent trail that invites predators like raccoons to check your boxes for you, with disastrous results. Predator guards mounted over the nest box hole give little or no protection. But a box mounted on a metal pipe that's fitted with a predator baffle can be monitored without fear of such a tragedy.

It's helpful to know what to expect when you open a box. Here's a timetable that tells how long an average bluebird pair spends at each nesting stage:

Nest building:	1-6 days
Egg laying:	5-7 days
Incubation:	eastern: 14 days
	mountain: 13-15 days
	western: l4 days
Brooding:	6 days (all species)
Fledging:	eastern: day l6-21
	mountain: day l9-23
	western: day l9-22

Properly mounting your bluebird boxes on metal poles fitted with 24-inch stovepipe or 30-inch conical metal baffles will prevent depredations by climbing predators. Situating boxes 25 feet or more from shrubs or trees will make them less attractive to house wrens. Still, there can be problems. On the following pages is a troubleshooting table, which will help solve most of the common "whodunits" on the bluebird trail. ➤

Nesting Schedule

In some cases, you may not know the hatch date of the young, and may need to estimate their age. This table gives some guidelines:

Day 1:	Bright coral-pink skin, eyes sealed, down in sparse tufts.
Day 2-4:	Wings, head, spine look bluish due to developing feathers under skin.
Day 5-7:	Feather sheaths begin to emerge on wings. Eyes still closed.
Day 7:	First feathers burst from tip of sheaths. Eyes open as slits. Brooding by female stops.
Day 8-11:	Eyes fully open. Feathers continue to burst sheaths.
Day 11-12:	Feathers of wing and tail reveal cobalt blue in males, duller gray-blue in females. Female eastern bluebirds show white edging on outer tail feathers.
Day 13:	Cut-off date for box checks. Fully feathered young become increasingly active, and may fledge prematurely if box is opened.
Day 16-22:	Fledging and first flight. Empty nest soiled, flattened. Young remain in cover while parents bring food.
Day 28 on:	Fledglings fly strongly, following parents who feed them.
Day 35 on:	Fledglings feed unassisted.

Try to keep written records. Even if you monitor a single box, it's good to keep records and not trust your memory. It's important to know how old the young are to avoid causing premature fledging by opening the box after Day 13. Styles of record-keeping differ, but you'll want to record the following:

Date:	Weather, time.
Nest:	Note inches of material, whether cup is lined, condition after fledging.
Eggs:	Number, whether warm or cold.
Young:	Number, age (count hatch day as Day 1) condition, sex of nestlings if desired.
Parasites:	Type, any countermeasures taken.
Fledglings:	Number, date of fledging if known, post-fledging sightings.
Comments:	Presence of adults, competitors, behavioral notes, other observations.

Most trail operators keep a spiral-bound notebook with a page for each box, and refer to the last entry before approaching a box.

Competitors

Sparrows, starlings, swallows, wrens, flycatchers, and even squirrels compete with bluebirds for nest cavities.

It's all too easy to become goal-oriented in bird watching, and to pass over some species in favor of other, "better" birds. Keeping nest boxes is subject to the same pitfall. A bluebird box should have bluebirds, the dogma goes, or we've failed. When I first started keeping boxes, I had this attitude, but I've come to appreciate other inhabitants

Tree swallows (above) and violet-green swallows will readily assume ownership of bluebird boxes.

(swallows, for one) as much as I do bluebirds, and they are just as welcome in my boxes.

A bluebird landlord should be conversant with federal law before setting out. Bird boxes should not be equal-opportunity housing. Certain species should be encouraged,

STEVE BYLAND

others left alone, and still others thrown out without ceremony.

Two species designated as undesirable aliens, having been introduced to this country, are the European starling and the house sparrow. Unprotected by law, they and their nests can be destroyed if necessary. Although the starling competes fiercely for natural nest cavities with larger entrance holes, it is too stocky to gain entry to a hole 1⁹⁄₁₆ inches or smaller, and so it rarely causes problems for box-nesting bluebirds.

House sparrows, on the other hand, are smaller than bluebirds, and can't be stopped from entering boxes. There, they throw out bluebird eggs and young, and sometimes trap and kill adult bluebirds on the nest. Try never to allow house sparrows to use a box. Throw out their nesting material, which includes weed seed heads, feathers, straw, and trash in an arc curving up the back of the box.

Trap the adults if you can. One sneaky way to do this is to allow the sparrows to build for a day or so, then to plug the box hole while the bird (preferably the male) is inside. You can do this after dark, if the bird is too wary. Then, secure a plastic bag or pillowcase over the box hole, unplug it, and nab the sparrow as it exits. Unprotected by law, house sparrows may be destroyed, or relocated miles away.

If you've a number of sparrows to remove, visit **nabluebirdsociety. org** to order traps. Overall, however, it's best to avoid putting up boxes near barnyards where animals are fed, for house sparrows are dependent on a steady source of grain. Fighting them in such

CALIBAS/WIKI

ALAN VERNON/WIKI

A house wren (top) and house sparrow (female, bottom). Both species will evict bluebirds and destroy their nests.

situations can be an exercise in futility, and lead to unnecessary loss of bluebird nests and lives.

Native species attempting to nest in bluebird boxes should,

Continued on page 18.

PROBLEM	LIKELY CAUSE	SOLUTION
Box filled with unorganized twigs. Eggs pierced and/or on ground below box, leaving nest undisturbed. Nestlings pecked on head or dead on ground below box, nest undisturbed.	HOUSE WREN	Keep twigs removed. Plug hole until wren relocates. Mount wren box with 1-inch hole near shrubbery. Move bluebird box 100 feet away from shrubs, trees. Leave completed wren nests alone, and erect another box in the open for bluebirds.
Box filled with straw, trash, feathers, curving up back of box. Eggs missing or on ground below box, nest undisturbed. Nestlings pecked on head or dead on ground below box, nest undisturbed. Adult bluebird dead on nest, head pecked.	HOUSE SPARROW	Allow bird to build, then trap by plugging hole. If this fails, use trap in box or cage trap baited with cracked corn. Destroy or relocate birds miles away. Don't mount boxes near barns where animals are fed; don't feed corn. If sparrows outnumber bluebirds, accept defeat and remove boxes.
Feathers, often white, on top of nest. Rarely, eggs missing or young pecked, nest undisturbed.	TREE SWALLOW	Erect another box 15-25 feet away. Tree swallows are to be welcomed as nesters, will help defend bluebirds from wrens, sparrows, other swallows.
Female bluebird, eggs or young gone; nest pulled out of hole, feathers on ground under box. Scratch marks on box.	RACCOON, HOUSE CAT, OPOSSUM, OTHER MAMMALS	Clean box and remount on metal pole fitted with predator baffle. Mount in open area, far from cover.
All eggs or young gone, nest undisturbed, no scratch marks on box or remains left.	RAT SNAKE	Remove nest. Remount box on pole fitted with stovepipe predator baffle.
One or more eggs or young missing, nest undisturbed, no scratch marks or remains left.	CROW, GRACKLE, MAGPIE	Install 3/4-inch wood predator guard over hole. Lower nests built right up to hole by removing an inch or two of material from the bottom. For chronic magpie problems, use sheet metal extension to lengthen roof overhang to 5 inches over the hole.

PROBLEM	LIKELY CAUSE	SOLUTION
Adults flutter at box hole but don't go in; nest may be abandoned though pair seen in the area.	WASPS, BUMBLEBEE	Check inside ceiling of box for wasp nest. Crush nest and insects with long stick (wait until dark if insects are aggressive.) Rub bar or liquid soap on box ceiling to repel. *Don't use insecticides in box.*
Nest infested with ants.	ANTS	Remove broken eggs or dead young. Replace nesting material if young are threatened. Apply a band of grease, oil, or teflon spray to pole.
Nestlings weak and slow to develop, heads and wings scabby. Maggots may be attached under wings. Dirty, ill-smelling damp layer under nest cup. Brown pupal capsules in bottom of box.	BLUEBIRD BLOWFLY	Use putty knife to check under nest cup. Remove and confine nestlings, remove nest, clean box. Pack fresh dry grass tightly in box and replace nestlings. *Do not use insecticide in box.* Do not attempt blowfly control after nestlings are 13 days old.
Nestlings dead or chilled in wet nest.	HYPOTHERMIA	Check boxes often in cold, wet weather. Fill vent holes with putty-type weatherstripping (Mortite). Replace wet nest with clean dry grass. Remove dead nestlings, and warm living ones before replacing. Supplement food with mealworms or scrambled eggs placed in a jar lid duct taped to the box roof.
Apparently healthy nestlings found dead, unmarked but bloated, often about 8 days old, parents in attendance. Parent disappears without signs of predation. Birds found dying with tremors, disorientation.	PESTICIDE/HERBICIDE POISONING	Investigate nearby gardens, lawns, golf courses, roadsides, powerline cuts for brown, withered vegetation (herbicide) or signs of pesticide use (lawn care company signs, excessively manicured lawns or gardens). Try to arrange a moratorium on spraying. Relocate box if unsuccessful. Never erect boxes where lawn care chemicals are used.

under federal law, be left undisturbed. This includes tree and violet-green swallows, and all chickadees, titmice, nuthatches, wrens, and flycatchers. Target bluebirds by placing boxes at least 25 feet from trees and shrubs. Of native species, only swallows generally prefer the same open habitats that bluebirds do.

Where tree swallows are plentiful, they give stiff competition to bluebirds, sometimes ganging up on a pair to drive them away. Bluebirds largely avoid such competition by starting their nests several weeks earlier than do tree swallows. Wet, cold spring weather, though, can delay bluebird nesting until swallows swing into gear. When this happens, it's best to put up another box or two, to ease the pressure. Mounting boxes in pairs, l5 to 25 feet apart, can satisfy both species. Often bluebirds will settle in one and swallows in another, a setup that can benefit the bluebirds. Swallows will defend **both** boxes from other swallow pairs, as well as dive-bombing any other competitors or predators that approach. Trusting and beautiful, tree swallows go about their business in our presence, peering up from drifts of white feathers that line their nests, their flat little heads peeking comically from entrance holes. Their nests should be monitored just as those of bluebirds are. Swallow young are often staggered in size. Smaller young may perish, and dead nestlings should be removed.

Carolina, Bewick's, and house wrens may all occupy bluebird boxes, but only the house wren regularly evicts bluebirds by destroying their eggs and young. Though house wrens are protected by federal law and nests with eggs should be left undisturbed, "dummy nests," made by the male and composed of unorganized sticks, may be removed to give bluebirds another chance. One male house wren may fill several nest boxes with dummy nests, rendering them unfit for any other species. For wren problems, it is best to keep boxes 100 feet or more from cover. Plugging the hole temporarily may encourage a persistent wren to set up housekeeping elsewhere. Once wrens have settled and laid eggs, they must not be disturbed — they'll "retaliate" by destroying the nearest bluebird or swallow nest and moving into it.

Mammalian competitors include white-footed and deer mice, which make fluffy nests in boxes in winter but rarely return if removed in early spring. Flying squirrels may usurp boxes fewer than 100 feet from tall trees, and may prey on bluebird eggs and young. In many areas of the country, these beautiful squirrels are threatened, and should be discouraged if necessary only by relocating boxes to open areas. Chipmunks and mice, which climb to boxes, can be stopped with predator baffles designed for snakes and raccoons. Wondering who you'll meet when you open a nest box is part of the fun of monitoring. 🐦

How to Baffle Them

Predators

Simple things you can do to predator-proof your boxes

Picture a perfect farm scene, and it might include bluebird boxes on fence posts, or nailed to the old apple tree. I learned the hard way that both these classic methods of mounting nest boxes create potential deathtraps for bluebirds. Thirty years ago, my first bluebird boxes were nailed to trees in my yard. All went well that first year. But the second year, the local raccoons and black rat snakes learned that an easy meal awaited them in my boxes, and a brooding female and several broods of young went to them instead of into the skies.

Many people who have a number of bluebird boxes to monitor consider predation a natural part of the scene, which, of course, it is. But a distinction should be made between bluebirds that nest in natural cavities and those attracted to artificial sites. How many times have you walked right past a woodpecker hole high in a tree and never noticed it? Can you say the same of a nest box mounted on a tree, fence post, or pole?

Now imagine you're a grizzled old raccoon or black rat snake, veteran of many years of searching for birds' nests hidden in almost every imaginable situation. You know to watch for parent birds carrying food, to listen for or sense the shrill pipings of nestlings. Just once, you follow these cues to a wooden box, and are richly rewarded for your climb. A meal, and

A hole-mounted predator guard does not deter a bull snake from preying on a mountain bluebird nest.

ENJOYING BLUEBIRDS MORE

19

How to Make the Gilbertson Baffle & Pole Mount

Materials used: aluminum electrical conduit ½" diameter x 5' long, #4 iron rebar ½" x 5' long, two ½" conduit connectors, two ¾" machine screws (flat head), ½" strapping brackets and weatherproof screws (to mount box to pole), duct tape, hanger iron (in two 7" strips) or hose clamp, two machine screws with nuts for hanger iron, galvanized stovepipe (34" x 6") with 6" steel cap, and a knockout punch for ½" conduit (hole .89 ½") to make a neat hole in the stovepipe cap to accommodate the pipe.

Buy ½" aluminum electrical conduit and ½" iron rebar in a 10' length and have it cut at the store or cut it with a hacksaw into two 5' lengths. This will make two pole setups. With a mallet, drive one 5' length of iron rebar halfway into the ground. Slip one 5' length of conduit over the rebar; the rebar serves to support the conduit. Drop a ½" conduit connector over the top of the rebar, and replace the lower screw in it with a ¾" machine screw. This connector serves as a sleeve to affix the conduit firmly in its supporting rebar, and it prevents swiveling. Tighten both screws down—the lower screw into the rebar and the top screw into the conduit.

Using the knockout punch, make a hole in the center of the stovepipe cap. Bend and crimp the stovepipe into a cylinder. Fit the cap into the knurled end of the stovepipe.

Hold box up at height it will be mounted. A few inches beneath the box, run a double strip of duct tape around the conduit pipe. Bolt the two strips of hanger iron securely around the duct tape, on either side of the mounting pipe, and bend them as shown. Slip the assembled baffle over the top of the pipe and down to support the hardware cloth. Duct tape wrapped around the pole helps hold the hanger iron in place (A hose clamp will also work). Slip the assembled baffle over the hanger iron bracket, just below where the nest box will hang (the higher on the pole, the better). It should wobble a little, which further discourages climbing predators. Mount the nest box using the strapping brackets. You're done!

The slick metal baffle wobbles on the pole, preventing snakes and climbing animals from reaching the box. Baffle pole and mount designed by Steve Gilbertson, whose sparrow-resistant PVC and wooden Gilbertson boxes mount without hardware on ½" electrical conduit. Boxes are sold by Merlin Lehman, 60026 County Rd. 35, Middlebury, IN 45640-9750 • Ph: 574-825-8739.

packaging, to remember. And the nest boxes in your territory become predator feeders.

In attracting bluebirds away from cryptic natural cavities to conspicuous nest boxes, we are in a sense setting them up for predation. The incubating female, potential mother to dozens of offspring, might slip unnoticed into a tree hole, but less secretly to a box out in an open field. She is at special risk, and her death impacts the breeding potential of a local population.

Should we put up nest boxes at all? Yes, but only if we accept the responsibility that goes with them, to monitor and protect them from predators.

As I continued to work with bluebirds, my learning curve continued to rise, albeit slowly. Reluctant to take my boxes down, I took the easy way out. I put hole-mounted "predator guards" on the boxes, a 1-inch thickness of wood that effectively deepened the box entrance to 1¾ inches. In theory, a raccoon would be unable to reach through this thickness and then down to grab the birds. No one told the 'coons, though, and if it was a little harder to get the reward, they simply kept at it, or chewed the guard off. Needless to say, the snakes were unfazed. I thought about the terror a mother bird must experience as a raccoon chewed its way through her door, and I decided that mounting a predator guard on a box hole is like putting an ambulance at the bottom of a cliff. Once the predator is on the box, there's very little hope for the bluebirds inside.

Off came the boxes on trees and fence posts. Out to the plumber's

supply to buy pipe and strapping brackets to be screwed into the back of the boxes. I settled on 30-inch conical sheet metal baffles, kept in place under the box with hose clamps above and below the baffle neck. The predation stopped cold, and maintaining bluebird boxes turned from a guiltfest into the pleasure it ought to be.

The big baffles had some drawbacks. They had to be removed at the end of nesting season, lest they self-destruct in winter winds. The boxes had to be removed to take them off. They were big and cumbersome. Baffles made of plastics—even those sold as ultraviolet resistant—simply broke down in sun and freezing temperatures.

I decided to run tests of other baffles. I began setting table scraps out on a platform bird feeder, and soon raccoons were coming nightly. They climbed the galvanized pipe with ease. Grease did nothing to stop them, for it soon hardened and got sticky. (Even fresh grease won't stop snakes). Wide-circumference PVC pipe was easily climbed; the racoons simply gave it a bear hug and shinnied up. The same went for a cedar post wrapped with sheet aluminum.

Finally, I found a baffle that worked, that was easy and cheap to make, and that didn't have to be removed. It's just a 24-inch section of galvanized stovepipe, 6 inches in diameter. For roughly $10, you can ensure safe nesting for bluebirds, and disappoint raccoons, snakes, cats, opossums, chipmunks, and mice. It should be mounted just under the box. ➤

Bluebirds are fastidious nest-keepers. Here a male eastern bluebird removes a fecal sac. But parasitic blowfly larvae avoid detection by emerging only at night.

Parasites and Insect Pests

BILL THOMPSON, III

Parasite control might be classified as one of the fine points of bluebird house management. As you become more involved in the lives and success of "your" bluebirds, the subtler points assume more importance.

Ants, lice, mites, and earwigs are rarely found in a box that is mounted in the open on a metal pole. Tree trunks are highways for parasites as well as predators, and should not be used for box mounting. Ant infestations can be controlled by replacing the nesting material, cleaning the box, and smearing a band of STP Oil Treatment or applying a teflon

A 13-day-old male eastern bluebird with blood-sucking blowfly larvae, pupal capsules, and adult parasitic blowflies. After day 13, nest boxes should not be opened as young may fledge prematurely.

coating (either teflon spray or teflon tape) around the pole. Mites, which can multiply to debilitating proportions, can be discarded with the nest, and the box dashed out with hot water. Replace the nest with fresh dry grass packed tightly into the box, and replace the young in the fresh material.

The bluebird blowfly (*Protocalliphora sialia*) looks like a bluebottle fly, with red eyes. The female lays eggs in the bluebird's nest, which quickly hatch into grayish maggots, each about the size of a navy bean. They crawl out at night (thus avoiding detection by the adult bluebirds) to drink the blood of the nestlings. While a light infestation involves less than 50 larvae, as many as 240 have been found in one nest. Infestations usually get heavier as the summer wears on; first broods of bluebirds are less prone to attack than later broods.

Blowflies are likely to seriously weaken nestlings only in the face of other stresses, like food shortages due to prolonged rain or drought. Several preventive measures have been suggested. A false floor of hardware cloth, creating a space between the nest and box floor, is often used. Larvae which drop through the mesh would, in theory, be unable to crawl back up. Most larvae, however, live just under the nest cup while actively feeding on the nestlings, and only crawl to the bottom when ready to pupate. At this point, the damage is already done, as pupae and adult flies do not feed on blood.

Many sources recommend the use of pesticides such as rotenone or the supposedly safe pyrethrins, applied to the nesting material. But controlled studies have been done largely only on captive canaries and chickens, which are subject to few of the stresses and energetic demands of wild bluebirds. Nestling bluebirds, with their tissue-thin skins and high metabolisms, are extremely sensitive to toxic compounds, and in this case, the cure may

well be worse than the parasite! A tiny parasitic wasp *(Nasonia vitripennis),* that preys on blowfly pupae, would also be killed by insecticides. The safest option is replacing the infested nest.

If you decide to monitor your boxes for blowflies, you'll need to know the exact age of the nestlings. Those that are 9–11 days old are ideal. After Day 13, you run the risk, in opening the box, of causing them to fledge prematurely.

To check for blowflies, separate the nest material just under the

Bluebird Rescue

There will be times as a bluebird landlord when you hit a wall. Either way you go, you may be doing the wrong thing. One of the tougher dilemmas is presented by orphans.

Here's what to do if you find bluebirds that you believe to be orphaned.

First, make sure neither parent is tending the box. This is best done with a continuous watch from a distance. If no adult visits within four hours, you may assume there's trouble. However, if only one parent appears to be tending the young, it may be able to raise them unassisted. If the male disappears, the female will be able to raise the young, for she will brood them at night. The male bluebird, though, lacks this instinct, and though he will feed the young, he won't brood them overnight. He'll be able to keep them alive only if they are more than a week old, and the weather cup, and look for a soiled, smelly layer crawling with larvae. Check the bottom of the box for the larvae and their brown pupal capsules. If you see more than a few, the nest probably has a heavy infestation.

Gently remove the nestlings and place them in a bucket or box. Lift the infested nest on the putty knife, and drop it into a paper bag, scraping out any pupal cases on the box floor as well. Fashion a new nest from dry (not green) grasses, gathered in advance. Pack the grasses together tightly, with a cup to support the nestlings. Last, replace the young birds and retreat, watching from a distance to ensure that the parents return.

In most cases, replacing the nest is strictly optional, and the nestlings would, in all likelihood, fledge successfully without such measures. From my standpoint, there's no reason to allow mites or blowflies to weaken nestlings if I have the means to prevent it, so I go the extra mile as a bluebird landlord and replace the nesting material as needed. ✒

is warm. If the chicks are warm to the touch and seem well-fed, leave well enough alone. Take them in only if you're sure they're doomed otherwise.

Second, if you must intercede, warm the chicks up in a small cooler with a bottle filled with warm water. They won't be able to gape and eat unless they are warm.

Third, prepare emergency rations. Scrambled egg or canned dog food with egg yolk is a good, quick meal. Mold it into small balls, and with tweezers or a blunt toothpick push it gently into the birds' mouths to stimulate swallowing. A soft whistle may encourage them to gape.

Fourth, locate a licensed wildlife rehabilitator. It's illegal, not to mention difficult, to raise young birds, which need food every quarter-hour when small. They have a much better chance to survive with someone who has experience. Search the Internet for "wildlife rehabilitator" in your town

and state until you find someone who specializes in songbirds. Your state's nongame wildlife division should also keep a list of people with the proper permits for wildlife rehabilitation.

Fifth, try to locate a bluebird trail operator in your area. Someone with a sizeable trail usually has several boxes with birds the same age as your orphans. Fostering the nestlings to host nests is the best route of all. Local bird clubs, nature centers, or your state nongame wildlife division might be able to supply you the name of a trail operator in your state. It's worth the effort, for their best chance at a normal bluebird life is with real bluebird parents.

Bluebird Paradise

Enhancing your property for bluebirds.

ILLUSTRATION BY JULIE ZICKEFOOSE

O pen habitat is essential for bluebirds, which forage by sight, spotting insects from a perch and dropping down to snatch them. In the winter, they will flock and travel into wooded swamps for berries, but breeding birds need open fields and pastures, full of crickets, grasshoppers, spiders, and caterpillars, close to their nest sites.

Every time you mow your lawn, you are creating ideal foraging conditions for bluebirds. As the summer wears on and vegetation gets higher, it becomes increasingly difficult for them to find their ground-hugging prey. They are attracted to mown areas with plenty of perches from which to hunt.

One of the easiest, cheapest and most satisfying habitat enhancements you can make is putting up foraging perches. Dead tree limbs or garden stakes, with or without cross-pieces, are ideal. Scattered about your yard, perches open up new foraging opportunities for bluebirds, allowing them to feed throughout the expanse instead of just along the edges. You'll find lots of other species appreciate

On the raw edge of winter a pair of eastern bluebirds fills up on sumac fruits. A nest box will provide a snug roost as dusk comes on.

A mountain bluebird wing-waves as his mate chooses their nest site.

these perches; ours attracted great-crested flycatchers, phoebes, tree swallows, mockingbirds, and goldfinches, among others.

Water is another sure-fire attractant for bluebirds, who bathe lustily and often daily. They prefer a bath no more than two inches deep, with flat rocks creating varying water depths and a secure foothold. Natural tree branches arranged around a bath in the open enhance its attractiveness; birds are often leery of landing right on the bowl and need a perch from which to size it up. Most birds, in addition, find it hard to resist moving water. Whether you rig up a hose hung over the bath or use a recirculating pump, you'll be glad you did.

Bluebirds, with the exception of the mountain bluebird, are not strongly migratory; that is, they will linger in northern zones provided they have ample food. Although insects are taken on warm days throughout the winter, bluebirds rely largely on fruiting plants. The most commonly taken fruit in one study was sumac, which constituted 88 percent of the seeds regurgitated under a roost. Flowering dogwood, wild grape, Japanese honeysuckle, climbing bittersweet, multiflora rose hips, pokeweed, *Viburnum* species, greenbrier, and poison ivy are also taken. Many of these are considered troublesome weeds, but they sustain bluebirds throughout the winter.

Although I wouldn't recommend planting it, my opinion of poison ivy took a sudden turnaround this winter when I saw three pileated woodpeckers, together with hermit thrushes and bluebirds, dangling in a single huge poison ivy vine, eating its white fruits with obvious relish. Perhaps such plants should be allowed to prosper in

a forgotten corner, while the less invasive native species serve to bring bluebirds closer to the house.

If you regularly see bluebirds in your yard in winter, you may wish to try feeding them. Few of us think of bluebirds as typical feeder birds, as most feeding stations offer little to interest these insect and fruit-eating birds. However, in recent years increasing attention has been given to bluebird feeding and feeders.

The trick in attracting bluebirds to a feeder is to lure them in with some conspicuous natural food, such as a branch of climbing bittersweet or flowering dogwood in fruit. Draping this around a simple platform may bring bluebirds in to a feeder, where other foods can be offered to tempt them. Mealworms can be offered in low glass dishes that aren't obtrusive but that serve to contain the insects. Dogwood fruits, which can be gathered and

Improved Zick Dough

Combine and melt in the microwave or over low heat:
- 1 cup peanut butter
- 1 cup lard

In a large mixing bowl, combine:
- 2 cups unmedicated chick starter (available at farm/feed stores)
- 2 cups quick oats
- 1 cup yellow cornmeal
- 1 cup flour

Add melted lard/peanut butter mixture to the combined dry ingredients and mix well. When cool, crumble and serve in a shallow dish, protected from rain.

Store in peanut butter jars. Does not require refrigeration.

This food should only be offered in cold or inclement weather, because it is rich.

Water is an excellent way to attract bluebirds. Here a male eastern bluebird enjoys a favorite water feature in the author's backyard.

frozen for later use, can be mixed with crumbled suet and chopped, soaked raisins. Some people report success with sunflower chips and hearts, or peanut hearts.

Once bluebirds are coming to your feeder, you may find that a mockingbird or starling flock keeps them from using it. At this point, a bluebird feeder is in order. You can retrofit an old nest box with a shelf inside, just under the hole, on which to put the food.

More advanced feeder designs look like covered bridges, with 1½-inch holes in either wooden end and Plexiglas sides. The clear sides allow bluebirds to see the food, and the entry holes exclude starlings and mockingbirds. Feeder owners caution that you should check them frequently, since some bluebirds may try to exit the feeder through the transparent sides, rather than the entry holes. (See "Resources" for ordering information.) 🐦

JULIE ZICKEFOOSE

Planting for Bluebirds

This chart features native North American trees, shrubs, and vines which benefit bluebirds as well as other bird species. Adapted from tables compiled by Karen Blackburn for the North American Bluebird Society. (Reprinted from Sialia Vol. 13:3, 99-103). M,F= Male/female plant required.

TREES

Common Name	Latin Name	Fruiting Time	Height	Hardiness Zone	Comments
Cedar, E. Red	Juniperus virginiana	F,W	50' max	2	Year-round cover, winter food.
Cedar, Rocky Mt.	J. scopularum	F,W	50'	2	As above. Several other Juniperus species used.
Cherry, Black	Prunus serotina	S	50'	3	These summer-fruiting trees attract 50 bird species.
Cherry, Pin	P. pensylvanica	S	25'	2	
Chokecherry, Common	P. virginiana	S	25'	2	
Dogwood, Alternate-leaf	Cornus alternifolia	F	30'	4	35 bird species use fruit of dogwoods.
Dogwood, Flowering	C. florida	F,W	30'	5	Ornamental. 40 bird species attracted to fruit.
Hackberry, Common	Celtis occidentalis	F	50'	5	Several related spp. also attractive to birds
Holly, American	Ilex opaca	F,W	50'	6	Prefers moist shade. M, F required. Excellent food.
Mountain Ash, American	Sorbus americana	F,W	30'	2	Bright orange fruits very attractive to many birds.
Tupelo, Black	Nyssa sylvatica	F	100'	5	Prefers moist soil. M,F needed.
Mulberry, Red	Morus rubra	S	70'	6	Fruits attract 40 bird species.
Sassafras	Sassafras albidum	S,F	100'	5	Fruits, cavities attract bluebirds.
Shadbush, Serviceberry	Amelanchier laevis	S	30'	5	Attracts 35 bird species. Related species useful.

SHRUBS

Common Name	Latin Name	Fruiting Time	Height	Hardiness Zone	Comments
Bayberry, Northern	Myrica pensylvanica	F,W	8'	2	Sandy soil required.
Blackberry, American	Rubus allegheniensis	S	8'	2	Forms thickets which attract 150 species.
Black Currant, American	Ribes americanum	S,F	5'	5	Hosts white pine disease. Plant with care.
Blueberry, Highbush	Vaccinium corymbosum	S	15'	4	Requires acidic soil. Highly attractive to birds. Many related species also used.
Chokeberry, Red	Aronia arbutifolia	F,W	8'	5	Prefers moist soil.
Cranberry, Highbush	Viburnum trilobum	F,W	12'	2	Bright red berries, ornamental. Many related native species also useful. Shade-tolerant.
Dogwood, Gray	Cornus racemosa	F,W	10'	5	Thicket-forming, good cover.
Dogwood, Red-osier	C. stolonifera	S,F	15'	2	As above.
Dogwood, Silky	C. amomum	F	10'	6	Ornamental. Tolerates wet soil.

Continued on next page

SHRUBS (continued)

Common Name	Latin Name	Fruiting Time	Height	Hardiness Zone	Comments
Elder, American	Sambucus canadensis	S	12'	4	Thicket-forming.
Hercules' Club	Aralia spinosa	F	15'	6	Bizarre, thorny, compound leaves. Attracts migrant warblers, thrushes.
Holly, Deciduous Huckleberry, Black	Ilex decidua Gaylussacia baccata	F, W S	30' 3'	7 2	M, F required. Sandy, acidic soil required. Many related species.
Inkberry	Ilex glabra	F, W	10'	4	Thicket-forming. Acidic soil required.
Nannyberry	Viburnum lentago	F, W	30'	2	Fast-growing, shade-tolerant.
Pokeweed Rose, Pasture	Phytolacca americana Rosa carolina	S, F F, W	12' 7'	3 5	Perennial herb; dies back in winter. Abundant fruit. Long-lasting fruit. Related species valuable to birds.
Sumac, Smooth	Rhus glabra	F, W	20'	2	Thicket-forming. Fruits persist into spring. Vital bluebird survival food.
Sumac, Staghorn	R. typhina	F, W	30'	3	As above.
Winterberry, Common	Ilex verticillata	F, W	15'	4	Ornamental. Acidic, moist soil, M, F required.

VINES

Common Name	Latin Name	Fruiting Time	Hardiness Zone	Comments
Ampelopsis, Heartleaf	Ampelopsis cordata	F	5	Resembles grape vines.
Bittersweet, American	Celastrus scandens	F, W	2	Invasive.
Grape, Wild	Vitis sp.	F	Varies	100 species of birds eat wild grapes. Good cover.
Mistletoe	Phoradendron serotinum	F, W	6	Parasitic on oaks; local in South.
Virginia Creeper	Parthenocissus quinquefolia	F, W	4	Attracts 40 bird species. Ornamental fall color.